This book belongs to

_____ Iordan _____

"Homework tonight is to think up something exciting for your project. As you know, you may take the whole school year to work on your project. Then, in the last two weeks before the summer vacation, you will each do a presentation to the class," said Mrs. Smith.

I pushed back my chair slowly, and hung back, waiting for everyone else to rush through the door in their hurry to get home.

I remembered Creative Ninja's plane flying around the room, while the teacher had smiled, even as she shook her head.

Inspiration can come from anywhere.

Imagination Imagination comes from having time to explore and think.

Ideas come to everyone, but not everyone writes them down so it's important to make notes of your ideas whether you use them or not.

For a long time, I didn't say anything. I was thinking. Then, an idea came to me!

All year, I worked on the project, keeping it a secret from everyone - even Humble Ninja.

Everyone was very curious about my project.

Finally, the day had come. I set up the room with some help from my dad.

My project was going to be all about African big cats, but it wasn't just a spoken presentation.

Instead, I made realistic paper mâché models of all the big cats - life-sized ones! The whole class gasped when they saw them..

But that wasn't all I had done. Inside each model, I had carefully placed motion sensors and sound recorders so as soon as anyone got close to the animals they would roar, chirp, or growl.

It was as though real wild animals were in the classroom!

The class absolutely loved the presentation, and all of them said that they would never forget how to tell the difference between a leopard and a cheetah.

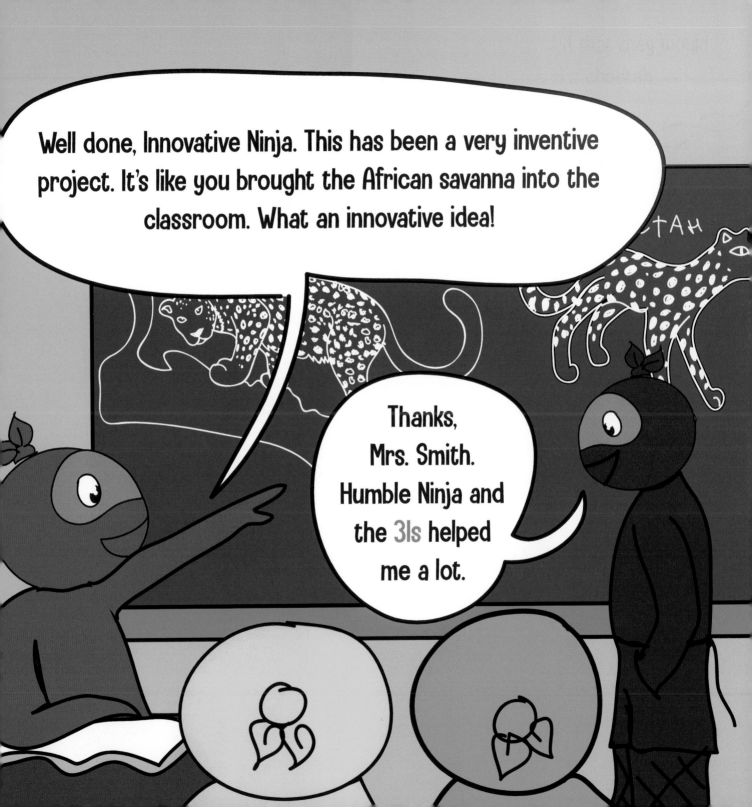

Remembering the 3 Is could be your secret weapon in building your innovation superpower!

Be sure to jot down your ideas in our Ninja Life Hacks Journal and Sketchbook!

@marynhin   @GrowGrit
#NinjaLifeHacks

Mary Nhin   Ninja Life Hacks

Ninja Life Hacks

Printed by Amazon Italia Logistica S.r.l.
Torrazza Piemonte (TO), Italy